Death and Life

Death and Life

By Peter Szabo

BP *Bloomingdale Press*
New York

For my family

CONTENTS

Death and Life

The Flood

Somewhere up in the mountains, it rains
 days and nights.
Dry creeks begin to flow,
down slopes, down ditches,
down gullies,
into streams,
 streams that find rivers.
In places not seen, a flood begins.

Rivers swell, angry
at nobody and everything.
Waters spill, up and over corroded banks,
searching,
 over the woodlands, the fields,
 over the streets, soon even the houses,
houses that, like boulders,
resist and embrace the torrent
with a splashing desire.

The flood rages.
Gentle surface swirls deceive,
obscuring the power of currents,
currents that scour the soil,
 hurl stones,
 rip up trees roots and all,
 pull down weak houses,
or just unlucky ones.
Unforeseen calamity reshapes everything.

Long after the waters recede
and the baked dirt cracks,
a restive doubt ebbs–

until the wind shifts,
the air thickens,
and the first cold drops darken desperate ground.

odyssey

When I opened my mind
and let you in,
you showed me the way to the door.
I did not want to go,
but I understood.

Monday, I had been parched
and bleary-headed. Still thirsty,
I grew focused,
though the drought seemed unending.

It was the end of many days of waiting.
On chill nights,
with a sharp moon high above,
I sat beside a mesmerizing fire
atop the hill next to the house
and stared into the emptiness.

The war had ended, but
the peace was not yet made.
There had been years of terror
and gore, when men of
different spirits tore
at one another with
divine ferocity.

Then, in the midst of our violence,
a rich and blinding mist
settled over the battlefield.
And the moss grew thick and soft
on the rocks and trees,
and men lay down

upon the cool, moist ground
and shut their eyes to dream.

I remembered that as a
boy I had loved trees, and often
made up tales of heroes and
beasts. Once, in make-believe
combat, I cut a tree with
a single swing of an axe. Seeing
it there, mortally wounded, I placed
it back upon the stump, and it
sprouted fragrant blue and yellow blossoms.

I arose. What I had left I
gave away or discarded.
Naked and penniless I
traveled footpaths that
took me from one kind
stranger to another, who,
in exchange for my stories,
gave me a hot meal and
a soft place to sleep.

I had been right as a boy:
life *was* mostly love.
For years I had convinced myself otherwise.
I arrived home.

The sun rose on Saturday
and the air shimmered
in a timeless heat.
By mid-morning Sunday
the flowers had died,
by afternoon the trees,
by evening
the children.

And so, when you knocked,
I knew there was nothing left to do
but answer.

Good-byes

They said you could slip any time,
  called without warning,
  told of your passing.

Without the chance to say good-bye
I'd not squeezed your hard hand,
  or heard the breathless wheezing
  or your see you soon.
I'd not seen your pain,
  or the pale, damaged body
  a tired soul made ready to abandon
  as defenses collapsed.

Eyes shut, I close our great distance.
Chuckles shared,
  rascal and stooge at play.
Denim palmed,
  a dark kiss dared.
Crew to your captain,
  counsel to your crisis.

We meet on memory's ground, alive,
the you I hold is flawed yet whole,
the I you touch asks, "Why that way?"
the air amidst grows warm and black.

Kaddish

To suck the succulent essence
of life from its insides,
lips closing hungrily
around the lamb bone,
   drawing out the small savory clump
   of marrow,
fingers coaxing the style slowly
from honeysuckle's flower,
   lips closing greedily
   around the sugar-dropped stigma

If the bead of nectar,
   or the pocket of nourishing paste,
is found only rarely
I will take heart from each find,
   fueled until the next
   by belief
   by passion-flash vision
for it was there,
and to give up expectation
to stop and settle
would be to taste less
to unlive

And when country lane
turns to dirt and disappears in bramble,
I will lie in the tall field-grass
rich with the smell of earth and plant
alive with wind and wing

Then take me
for I will have tasted forever

Bound

You run,
with the jumpy slaps
of a bongo player

You stand,
then melt
like a popsicle

You walk,
stretching each stride
like a Gillespie note

You stop,
the silence broken
only by your expectant smile

You sing,
an exclamation point
in an age of ellipses

When People Die

When people die
something is lost
Like a sock carried down to
  the laundry that now can't be found
Like a treasured title no longer
  in its spot on the shelf (Did I
  lend it to someone? Who?)
Like a guest who doesn't show up at
  a dinner party, doesn't even call with their
  regrets

When people die
their lives are over
Like the old clock that, having not been
  wound for ages, stops
Like a book closed upon its end
  with a thump
Like a damn good meal
  that leaves nothing lasting but
  the memory of its deliciousness

When people die
something breaks
Like the favorite vase that teeters
  from its pedestal and splashes upon the
  floor
Like an invisible chain
  that rattles and clangs as it
  slides noisily from around the iron
  bars of a life
Like my heart when I heard the news

When people die
our life begins anew
Its geology changes, and its
  landscape, and its climate
It changes direction, sometimes
  imperceptibly, sometimes in every way

And we select a few cherished items,
from among the too many,
that we fold and place neatly into
our pack
  before slinging it back onto our shoulders
  and taking the first tender steps forward

Exit

The newspaper said
they found your clothes in the tree,
between the roof
from which you had fallen
and the sidewalk
that killed you instantly.

A friend who had known us
in those molten teenage days
told me you slipped.
But what brought you to that edge?
The wine?
Your latest man?
The surprising spring snowfall?
Or your craving, manic heart.

I wonder what you thought about
as you charged through outstretched limbs,
resisting entanglement.

I know what I thought.
  Only you.

Whispers

The sun sets behind the mountain spine
that spreads hard against the close horizon.
Fluorescent ribbons of snow
disappear,
the faint glow of gray rock
dominates for a time,
before a speechless
call to pause, to see, appears
in rose-orange graffiti.
Then, stern darkness whitewashes it
from granite walls.

Camp chores call,
but tomorrow is a leaving day.
How departure arouses the past,
against our plans.

The gas-fire sky burns cool,
a dimming dance of blue and black.
Up and down the valley
sky simplifies to silhouette,
life's amplitude
set in a million years of stone.

The last pink of day–
a prayer of gratitude,
a prayer of hope.
For it whispers not from the highest peak,
it whispers from the lowest.

Self-Portrait of a Time

Born three weeks before President Kennedy
was shot.
Reared as the teargas fog descended
amidst the shooting
and looting and shooting and dying,
but mostly the shouting.

Not long after, the shadow-faced man
crept along the track,
pulled the switch,
and the train of desire,
that throbbing iron-elephant train,
took the branch it had not intended to travel,
and, as it picked up speed,
 whipped steamy cries
 into buttery thoughts.

The children left the front lines one by one,
laid down their posters,
unlocked their arms,
and floated off,
limp,
in body bags of sorrow.

Growing into wide-bottomed jeans that
opened like flowers upon happy feet,
we drew hope and peace on our bodies,
and on our clothes and our possessions,
in passionate colors,
foam from the crashed and spent wave,
the acid wave,
the Technicolor foam,
spreading and folding,

stroking the backs of our necks,
like a loving mother.

In the creek we slipped and laughed
and pointed and shushed
as we looted minnows and tadpoles and frogs
and brought them to leaky backyard ponds,
hastily dug.

One leader frightened, the other fizzled,
bookending a long decade.
I rolled over in the hazy dawn,
the gray light casting a shadow
upon my dusty, honeycombed mind.
Something had changed,
ended, like all youth.

The charming man's smile turned everyone to plastic,
cut dreams into credit cards.
We followed his Pied-Piper voice
to money-den marshmallow roasts,
and shrugged, as he did,
at the grahamcrackerless.

I watched the lively campfire scene
from outside the ring,
wondering where I was,
smelling of ashen logs,
lost and burned,
dizzy, but even the dizziness
was mostly gone,
gone with the fog and smoke.

Maturing as a new youth pushed us aside
with great greedy heaves,
hard to our ambivalent avarice.

They spoke at one another,
then the rest of us,
with enraptured indifference,
while a blossom blew off and up,
looping, spinning, whirling away,
unable to wait any longer.

Alive the day the grass, the plants,
the trees, the streets, the buildings,
the city, the river,
the land, the oceans, the air,
the earth,
became just a fraction of a degree
warmer.

The fall of our time in the breeze,
but still not aware
that life floats away from us
one crispy brown leaf at a time.

A Dying Fire

Everything in the world is gray
gray as the smoke of a dying fire
or a somber mist blown in from the sea
Even in bright sun
  even in bright spring sun

Walls thin
crack
dissolve
Every way is forward
Whispers
  "impossible"
I go nowhere
stiffen
blink

I clench numb fingers
  open them
wiggle senseless toes
No more alone
in a silent wilderness
than in a crowded room

Hope yesterday
  but I cannot recall what for
Will
  but now only its residue remains
Everything I was
everything I wished to be
  mix
And I am less and less sure
who I am

There is nothing to be done for me
 I am not drowning
No one can understand
 what I am is all I have
Down to a final thought

          A breeze wafts away the gray
          Dry air depletes the dampness
          On a warm clear morning
          I pause before a garden
           ablaze with summer flowers

Collapse

From where I stood
somewhere below Broome Street
it looked like confetti,
tossed by the cheering
handful over the parade
of police and fire battalions
and the office workers
who streamed up lower Broadway.

For a moment
I smiled at the sight,
the confetti glittering
in the sun against an azure
September sky.

The dull smile
a barricade against the
fact that it was not confetti,
it was shards.
Glass shards.
Paper shards.
Steel shards.
Body shards.

Fortune Cookie

Of all the kaleidoscopic
mongrel muses who might
have lit my way,
your calliope laugh and
Bugs Bunny grin were not
what I'd expected.

But now I was dancing.
The Horah. The Rumba.
That crazy Cossack dance
where they squat and kick
their legs out.

And magic tricks
I'd never imagined
passed through me
daily. I made
Lady Bird flowers
bloom on asphalt,
and old rail yards
I turned into Luna Parks.

I played loud sweet notes
on strange instruments
and filled the wilds
with tunes of joy.
Animals came,
and we sang arm-in-arm
all night long.

I was psychic.
I dined with departed
grandparents,

hung out with long-lost
Huck-and-Tom friends.

I flew,
my fingers touching
the soft tops of pine trees,
and landed effortlessly
on Wright Brother dunes.

Nothing could hold me.
Not cuffs and ropes and
iron tanks filled with
water and welded shut
and fired into outer space.
I reappeared.

And then
I smiled,
god-like.
I remembered the time
in the Chinese restaurant
when you passed me
that fortune cookie,
eyes aglow.

It was all your doing.

The Swarm

There are so many ideas
ideas ideas ideas

Bursting out of my mind
Bursting out of my nerves
Bursting out of my skin

Pricking me, pestering me
Taunting me (with their attitudes)
Tormenting me (with their anticipation)
Tiring me out (with their assaults)

Crushing me beneath their weight
(I can hold them up no longer)
Swarming until I am provoked
(I wave at them frantically)

Impatient as children
They are so impatient

Days Like This

Days like this set one to wondering
whether what awaits is
eternal summer
or endless winter.

There
is there
a wildflower-speckled meadow
stretching before us
shaggy green grass shooting pink
and yellow and red knee-high sparks?
Do we experience the satisfying warmth
of sun on skin
hopeful birdsong and leafy applause
amplified in a gentle breeze
causing within us inexhaustible euphoria?

There
are there
ice-coated sidewalks
slush-filled street-corners
charcoal gray buildings and stone gray sky?
Does the bone-cracking chill penetrate until
we want to scream
and do the blank faces all around
and empty words everywhere
and the endlessness
the meaninglessness
feed within us
hopelessness
boundless hopelessness?

Maybe the need to know that it
is one or the other
is what makes us so here.

For maybe it is both,
like here only
without us.

Ship

Up on the lighthouse rail I pace
staring through my boots
stiff and cracked
worrying over and over my troubles
like a wave breaking again and again
over black and slippery rocks
never changing them.

Wondering why
we aspire to so much
yet leave so little of meaning
I lift my face into icy
gusts that lash my skin
and blow breathy laughter in my ears
while below
the sea slams
indifferent.

I follow the charcoal sea
slashed by wind-ripped whitecaps
to where it meets the gray sky
and watch the outlines of a freighter
move imperceptibly
forward
out of duty or despair
and disappear slowly
into an approaching fog.

Arms of Light

Into an oracle
phantasmagorical
phone booth once you crammed,

> then out you pressed
> in a yawn-smile dressed
> and into cacophony blammed.

Past nut-spangled trees
in a peach-petal breeze
you hopped, sashayed, and whirled,

> wearing wide pants and incense
> chanting fruiten repentance
> two old wooden canes you twirled.

The sky turned lime green
had a purple-pink sheen
it rained apple blossoms all night,

> awake the morning after
> the clouds crashed with laughter
> and threw off a tongue-flapping light.

A gal and a lad
both clad in plaid
hummed by an almond-top pond,

> in a circle joined hands
> then melted to sand
> and left but a twelve-bar band.

A flock of canaries
bouquets of rosemary
a thicket of oak spruce and cherry,

elected you king
presented a ring
in a shower of electric-red berries.

With clucking giggles
random escalator wiggles
the houses leaned over to whisper,

cross-legged kneeful
wide-armed and gleeful
you spun a bright mongrelized twister.

Death and Life

Red newborn eyes
search unseen skies,
death and life
death and life

Carnival dreams
morning thread beams,
death and life
death and life

A quetzal breeze
brass symphonies,
death and life
death and life

Cricket moist grass
scents sassafras,
death and life
death and life

Spring green love food
fall leaf crunch brood,
death and life
death and life

Wobble stone creek
towel soft cheek,
death and life
death and life

Barren white oak
breaths acrid smoke,
death and life
death and life

The skin grows pale
the long exhale,
death and life
death and life

Thin echo calls
canyon mist falls,
death and life
death and life

Freight train whistle
rumble whistle,
death and life
death and life

Young angel eyes
smoldering wise,
death and life
death and life

In circles round
the balls redound,
death and life
death and life

In circles round
the balls redound,
death and life
death and life

Spring Day

I carried you
piggyback
down the block
Jeans on my forearms
    smooth
Fleece around my shoulders
    warm
Cheek pressed against my neck
    soft
Sun on my face

A cool breeze filled the space
around us
But not between us
And though we parted on that
Spring day
Our shadows remained one
    Then our hearts
    Now our lives

New York City Subway Car

It's 9:30 on a Tuesday night and *damn* this Bronx-bound
#3 train is *crowded*.

There's a young black woman in a red leather jacket
and a matching red leather hat.
She's talkin' to a grungy white guy with one of those
itty bitty beards.
Two guys thumb wrestle on in Spanish across from me
–a father and a son.
The girl with her ribs on my elbow is Asian.
Farther down two men joke about something
in the Arabic newspaper they're reading.
Standing to the left of me's a Pakistani dude,
his clothes from some other time, looking like a big old
wood-paneled station wagon.

A young white couple stands by the doors.
They're in uniform–
black shirt, black pants,
black shoes, black jacket.
She's got two nose rings
and on her head is a tight black ski hat.
But dangling from the top of it there's these two wooly balls!
They're yellow! That's it, man!
Those two goofy yellow balls!

It's a mixing bowl, this car, and we're the ingredients.
I'm just oil, but there's vinegar over there,
and next to him ginger and pepper and cumin.
Curry and coriander and Tabasco stand at the far end.
The doors open at 72nd,
new spices shake on,
and the flavor's like some sauce your mother never made.

A tough girl steps in.
A wide, blue headband holds back her frizzy red hair.
Her frown, and the earring in her lower lip, say
"Blow it out your ass!"
A man nearby pays her no attention.
He's reading "The World's Most Powerful Money
Manual & Course."
The brim of his cap matches his pout.

The car is so full,
the moment is so full,
I feel the top and sides of this city.

The Arabs turn the page of their paper
the tough girl checks her watch
the Pakistani man shifts his feet
I stand up and grab the pole to steady myself
the young couple kisses
the father and son laugh
the train slows
the doors slide back
I tumble out.

November

November is all bittersweet good-byes,
wine and amber confetti swirling as
autumn's heroes–the trees, the geese,
the chilly, mist-filled breeze–pass the
season's mantle to foul winter
  who waits
  impatiently,
  claws fumbling,
  grinning a black, sharp-teethful grin,
  bearskin parka folded
  neatly over one arm.

November is all piles,
of grass, as Indian Summer's
  mellow gusts caress yellow-green lawns,
  and ten thousand thousand tiny hands extend in gratitude
  and bow before the last egalitarian blade
  clips them stiff and short;
of leaves, which
unclench themselves from springsummer homes,
  twirl and tumble to the ground, and
  holler yellowredorange hallelujahs in great rakish revivals;
of snow, when the North Wind enters
  without so much as a knock, scans the warm room
  full of guests and happy conversation, scowling,
  and exits
  scattering great fistfuls of his tiny white calling cards
  as he walks steadily home, pausing only
  to throw back his head in a frigid
  I'llbeback howl.

November is all humility,
a perpetual ending,
  modest before those who hail its beauty,
  grateful for the bounty laid before it,
  silent on the eleventh hour of its eleventh day,
  listening for lost voices in frostcrunchy leaves;
a vital old man,
  looking back upon giddyspring and foolishsummer
  with a knowing halfsmile
  and toward winter not knowing what lies ahead,
  but steadied by satisfaction.

November is all hope,
  that the stream of life will thaw and flow,
  that the sun will shine and the colors shout,
hope that it will be this good again.

History

What history we fight over
as it layers and falls
layers and falls
compressing into gems
senseless rocks
and black air
drawing memory into rivers
drying jungles
prairies
deserts.

Strange flowers
excite passion and war.
But from capture
blooms escape
inevitably.

I find fear in the water
that soaks and returns
soaks and returns
instead of hope.

Graveyards
hidden in courtyards
gather silence.
I walk by them
on the noisy avenue
not listening.

The scales of art
justice and time elude.
And the tingling air
will either save me or kill me
save me or kill me.

Canyon

Barren, our city view,
a dull collage of
windows, bricks, and
concrete,
deep as a canyon,
that shields the land,
the river,
even the sky,
from view.

The palette runs
brown to grey,
but for the square
inch of green in
our once-empty window box.

Tiny cup-like leaves
wait patiently for droplet gifts
from above.
Sporophytes
reach up and launch
seeds into swirling surface winds.

Blown in by unchartable currents,
dropped by bird or bug,
that square inch fills our canyon
with possibility.

Sixty Friends and Family

'Sixty friends and family,' she told me
as we sat on a park bench
one sterling Saturday.
Of their names I learned only two–
Simon
and Ishtvan.
'Ishtvan, that is Steven,' she explained.

They took the train
from Nagykanizsa
to Auschwitz,
along with their wives and children,
that awful spring.

She had a crush on cousin Ishtvan,
I could tell.
Her face brightened
as she told me the story of the time he crashed
his motorcycle while she rode in the sidecar.
Laughter shook her body,
and tears filled her eyes,
tears of mourning,
tears of love.

Of the others she said nothing.
I learned later that some took the highway
west from Budapest
to Mauthausen
that savage fall,
the blood of stragglers
reddening roadside snow.

What this meant to her
she would not say.
Only her voice hinted.

I wished for her a grand reunion,
imagined her with everyone
in a Beaux-Arts Budapest ballroom.
She mingles,
shares stories,
clinks glasses.
They dance.

Then I saw her
in her simple Queens apartment,
bringing her dishes to the sink,
and sitting down
in the La-Z-Boy
in front of the television
and its endless, empty applause,
alone.

Reconnaitre

You are off into the crisp afternoon
with a kiss and a distracted see you later
and I sit in dusk's dimness alone

It is quiet
Troubled thoughts lose their relationship
to you and stumble about
groaning stretching dazed
then sprint to the edges
of my mind
of my feelings
and back

Who will I be without you
as a muse
as a vessel
as an excuse

Like the paints you once smeared delirious
I thin and dissolve
into a faint hue
Like the books you once devoured ravenous
I grow infused
with staleness and dust
Diamond memories compressed from the
carbon of experience
return
each gem a different size and cut
yet refracting the same story
of me and you

"Hello," he says, startling me.
I had forgotten he was there.
His eyes, his voice,
are warm
and knowing.

Divide

Lines spill over eye's edge,
meandering like a river
through its delta end

Gray hair appears,
just one or two strands
Taught flesh softens,
becoming someone else's

Sweat saturates skin,
settling on the brow
as flush fades
Memory dries and flakes,
a dead-gray abandoned hive
Of its vast plumbing,
few trunk lines and feeders
function reliably

Experience cools ambition,
as the sea does flowing lava,
forming hard-yet-porous wisdom-stone

The soul crouches
amidst whistling ricochets,
near-miss concussions, collapsing structures
Brown-out hope flickers

The heart still beats,
sclerotic in parts,
fresh in others
Weakening physically, but pulsing
belief, love, courage
ever stronger

You tilt your head to
fasten an earring,
and your hair falls back
from your neck,
exposing the smooth nook
below the earlobe
where I still nestle

We reach our continent's divide
a hundred ridges around us
Clouds exhale at horizon's edge
where rivers of delight and sorrow
fill ancient seas

Gusts whisper encrypted secrets
we somehow understand
Your head inclines toward
the narrow, worn path that
winds to the tree line
Your face a blue eternity,
we step down

Fall Light

Light,
razor-sharp,
chisels
with a sculptor's single-mindedness.

Balustrades stand, march, breathe.
A stone lion roars, its claws gleam.
Sidewalks hug lamp posts,
and wrought iron fences.

Light illuminates cavities, skewed surfaces,
and obstacles with its absence,
giving the trees bravery,
the buildings a subtle wit,
the cobblestones, identity.

On a park bench I ponder the soul of such a creator.
The air hardens around me.
I pull my jacket tighter.
Light notices, and for as long as I sit
there is perfect balance,
cool air, warm light.

Walking home, I see light's golden lipstick
on the foreheads of old apartment houses.
Late now,
life pours in.

Some People Kill

Some people kill other people
because of the color of their skin
their beliefs
their clan
or for no reason at all

Some people hit their children
scream at them
abandon them

Some people shoot animals for fun
at close range
with automatic rifles
hovering in platforms
above a pile of bait
They bulldoze animal homes
or cage them
and drug and fatten them
so they can eat them

Some people sell people things
they do not need
tell them things that are not true
for money

Some people sit in traffic for hours
alone
every day
twice a day

We feel tethered to others
through the air
by little devices

and we communicate compulsively
trying to slake
our insatiable thirst for contact

We make war
we end war
having changed nothing
except the minds and limbs of
the combatants
and those caught in between

We break atoms
climb the tallest mountains
travel to the moon and back
build civilizations
and bring about their destruction

We light our homes
by means that poison our water
our air
our weather
no alternative found
or allowed
after years of trying
The warmest winter on record
and then it snows
and we go sledding
and forget

Death awaits
at the end of any one of a thousand roads
long or short
but we never speak of it
Meanwhile we love and betray
help and hinder
the same people

We work and laugh
while microbes rot and spoil our bodies
We have lovely songs in our hearts
but irregular voices

The struggle for meaning
ends in the folly
of a sanity of meaninglessness

Miracle

Graffiti appears on a subway wall
overnight
miraculously
Then disappears
under a coat of cream-colored paint
miraculously
overnight

Wave

I drive forward like a wave
feel its force behind me
in me
and find myself at its tip
as it begins to peak
the very tip
the front molecule
elastic and stretching

I am free
        free of worry
        free of guilt
        free of doubts and debts
        free of entanglements
There is no memory
There are no wishes

Everything is so alive
        greens of leaves and grass
        yellow to black-green
        blues of sky
        white to purple-blue
Those bricks
   I can see
   every grain of sand and mud
feel their roughness
with my eyes

My head is so crystal clear
it pops
   and cracks
like a hot glass suddenly filled
with ice cold water

over and over
it feels right

Everything is smooth
  simple
    certain
I know exactly what needs to happen
  what will happen
know it so completely
there is no knowing
no certainty
no means of describing
or doing
or being
it
only
it

And as I
  I guess
    think this
I exist in an ecosystem of peace
Mayhem
  tumult
shatter and swirl all around
But I am calm
a clear solid core
of a clear gelatinous world
that reverberates around me
but does not invade
my secure separate self

I see the whole and
a smiling serenity fills
me but does not overflow

I am tranquil
my soul is infinite
but cupped in my soft hands
I see the whole
        it is a terrified beast
        to be soothed
        cared for
        pitied generously
        and not feared
not a speck of fear
not a fleck of fear

It occurs to me that
whole
it is less troublesome
it is not troublesome
It sees me
in nonsensical fragments
through refracted light
I see it crystal clear

I move like a sharp-edged shadow
on a blinding-bright day
yes
    now
        to forge
walk purposefully
    surely to forge things through my will
yet my fist closes not upon real
objects to mold
to change
but
    upon nothing
    fruitless
as the wave passes its peak
frays as it falls

droplets charging madly
this way and that
  scattering
and then
          crash
and then
          silence
white
  foamy
    euphoric
      silence
        shhhhhhhhh

before the undertow
pulls me
  with a sand scraping exhale
  to distant applause
back out to sea

Holding Hand

You gave me that look today,
that look that says,
'I am not a boy.
I am a man.'

Still so young.
But I saw it there,
fleeting,
striking,
like the sliver flash of a fish
near the surface of dark water.

Instinctively
I glanced at the hand,
the hand that held
your naps on my chest
our footprints on the beach
aimless park days
stories
song.
Always holding on to me.

I glanced down at my
holding hand
realizing late
you had let go.

That look set everything ablaze.
And what uncertainty terrifies me
is whether we will find,
in conflagration's remains,
the ashes of an ink-filled diary,
or the charred conifer's progeny.

Feathery fibers
of memory,
or seeds
for hands to plant.

No. 57

In the square, a red light glows
disconsolately
Alone as a praying mantis
atop morning greenery
Isn't it lovely?
We filled up the car this morning
with four dollar gas
But all thoughts were of the subterranean
world where I dwell most
afternoons
My cousin, it was good to see him,
the old chap,
but not now
Today I have the part I used to play
and must be getting on
On the sidewalk
loafing
In the park
loafing
Dreaming a tree's dreams
of movement, of dance
Dreaming my father's dreams
They weren't so bad, crawling
around in the moonlight,
scattering
Howls of joy,
howls of joy,
bounce off tomatoes,
burrow into seeds
Why does the din and debris of a troubled
mind so resemble a whirlpool
swirling at that fiery joint between
the frothy wake and the undertow

Guidance. B train. Take the B to 59th
for goodness sake, it's faster
Faster, faster, faster, fast
Until the whirlpool sucks
it all in,
twisted sound and shattered light,
detritus
And there, on the trail of sense,
in a quiet
morning walking, just
walking,
I come upon it,
amidst vast acres of despair
My vernal pool of joy

From Now

I look at you
through a clear, soft
barrier
Impassible

A vague urge to
touch you
flickers
and then something like
a chuckle
diffuses through
me
the me best described
now as all that is not
physical

As I watch you plan
As I watch you work
As I watch you hurt
As I watch you laugh
As I watch you grow
colors within the now-me
swirl and change
grow brilliant
and dreamy
And what I used to feel
as emotion, now
tingles
prickles
thickens, and at the same time spreads

All the while
-though I cannot see it with eyes-
brightness, intensifying
Intensifying

To call this happiness,
to call this love,
would be as droplet to river,
flake to blizzard,
dawn to day,
touch to hold

And in these
-let us call them-
moments
something like a spark, a
molten drop,
separates, and
by divine mystery
travels,
as if through unseen
backstage passages,
to the you
inside you

I glow still brighter
by some means
beyond me,
and
our hearts touch,
as you think of me

To Roam

I remove the leash (I've never believed in cruel choke
collars) and my mind begins to roam.
A bus chuckles down the street and
coughs to a stop. It screeches at the light,
then rolls on its way.
My ears perk. Brakes? Or birds.
Birds, yes.
Birds in February?
Yes, birds, asking why, why, why? in clipped trills.
What notes are they playing?
G F#, G F# the calls,
B C, B C, the answer. B C.
A car starts, a drum roll.

Like a dog, my mind wanders
down to Riverside Park to relieve itself.
Obedient, yet primal.
Which to choose? Which to obey?
Primal wins. Primal always wins when the leash is off.
I trot around bare trees and across a green lawn
asleep beneath the snow, sniffing.

A low, wrought iron fence divides cultivated
garden, fallow now, from cultivated park.
Silly, boundaries. Especially boundaries
between like things.
That is where authority becomes despotic,
arbitrary, I bark.
On a leash like my dogmind, this park,
wanting to be wild, made so proper.

It's a long way to Harlan
It's a long way to Hazard
Just to get a little booze
Just to get a little booze

Music in my ears all morning, picking
strings made from my own gut.
I step onto the frozen Hudson
and climb aboard a tug which
nudges its way through the ice.

Down the Hudson! Down the Hudson!
(An ambulance giggles by)
Down the Hudson to the sea, man! I think,
as I stand on the path just above
the water, hands tight on the cold railing.
Railings, fences, silly boundaries.

In just a few months the trees will
spring leaves and the garden flowers will
jump up from the ground, spread their
arms and smile, like cheerleaders.
The air, now freshly milled steel,
will grow sweet.
Will I be dazzled by all this?
Or just bored.
Over and over again, the seasons.
Over and over again.

Up to the George and over the river.
You crossed the Delaware in a row boat,
I'll cross the Hudson on you!
On foot…Yes, on foot!
And I'll walk along hard highways,
into crackling forests, through soft
prairies and easy lumps of black soil

so tinglingly rich I can already
see the rows and rows and rows of corn
it will father, or mother.
Across the Plains and, with a great ladder, over the Rockies,
then down a river, any river, to the desert Northwest.
I'll take the stairs to the top of the Sierras,
then descend through the misty rainforest
(Goodness those trees are big)
to the islands, to the sea.
The sea!

Yes, across the land I'd roam.
Across, across, what draws me across?
The scent, the scent.

> *It's a long way to Harlan*
> *It's a long way to Hazard*
> *Just to get a little booze*
> *Just to get a little booze*
>
> *So roll on buddy*
> *Don't you roll so slow*
> *Tell me how can I roll*
> *When the wheels won't go*

I awake in the morning light, ablaze.
Flames, fueled by my heart,
consume my bones, lap at my eyes,
curl around my brain.

Awake minddog! Awake! I say.
I scratch behind my ears
and my leg begins to tap.
I lay still, warming myself by the fire,
listening to it snap and spark.

www.ingramcontent.com/pod-product-compliance
Lightning Source LLC
Chambersburg PA
CBHW031331040426
42443CB00005B/298